Finding a Voice

Shona Campbell

BookLeaf
Publishing

Presentation by *BookLeaf Publishing*

Web: www.bookleafpub.com

E-mail: info@bookleafpub.com

ISBN: 9789357440851

First edition 2023

To Erin and Jodie, my entire reason for being.

ACKNOWLEDGEMENT

Amanda for first suggesting I put my thoughts in writing. Leanne, Louise, Anna, Sonia and John for having to listen to my ideas but encouraging me to keep going nonetheless.

PREFACE

Meeting the many brave survivors of domestic abuse I learned how diverse their experiences were. Despite this diversity, there was a common theme of lack of understanding from others to the point of causing further pain. This misunderstanding often came from well meaning loved ones. I started writing in poetic form as a way to ease my frustrations at people's inability to understand survivor's experiences. These poems are the result

The Courthoose Staps

Aw life tae see amang the thrang
Lawer, assizer, and those they say did wrang
There's a feart witness, worrit, it's hard
At least there's the polis staunin guard
Inside sit the Shirras in wig and gown
Ready to announce if guid evidence has been
foun

Neervous fowk calm themsels wi a fag
Or try to look busy wi a tabloid rag
The time can be pit aff nae longer
Up tae the door we must wauner
Running the Gauntlet o aw the smeuk
Tryin no tae run intae fowk

Inside despite aw the fowk it feels sae quate
A warrant fur ye issued if ye be late
In front o the shirra an aith afore ye depone
Please nae be lang I wanna be gang home
Feels like hoors but it's soon ower
Back oot to the staps afore half fower.

How'd she No jist leave

Another wummin murdered it said on the news
Ye can't but help announce your views
 How'd she no jist leave ye rally the cry
Feel sae smug and awfie fly
The victim disnae hear, she'll hear nae mair
But yer loved ones will, is it really fair

If they find themsel in that situation, God forbid
They'll noo think twice afore the lift the lid
Ye see it disnae start wi a punch
But gifts, flowers and oot tae lunch
Then slowly but afore lang
Everything she does is Aeweys Wrang

By the time she gets to think a leaving
She remembers yer words when others were
grieving
Ye see he tells her they'll no believe ye,it's aw
yer fault
Remembering yer words thinks, aye they'd
agree a lot
So next time instead o prattling oan abit leavin
Why no think whit can a dae tae be savin

Leaving Time

It started with promises of love and hopes of
glee
But noo she feels she has to flee
No longer allowed a thocht o her ain
Never safe, especially at hame
He robbed her of her self-esteem, it's gone
Friends and family chased she's all alone

Call to the refuge no room at the inn
Funding's been cut it's such a sin
Next try the cooncil hameless team
An age for a call back it will seem
Finally on a train to a new destination
A free ticket to ride could be her salvation

Noo in her new room it wisnae easy
Sadly times will no yet be breezy
UC, find a job and maybe deal with polis
Start aw anew wi minimal help tae thole this
Looking ower her shouder, could he be here
Could spend the rest of her life dealing with the
fear.

The Escapee

In a controlling marriage she had been trapped
Her confidence, self esteem and energy sapped
Then she eventually got away
It should have been a celebration day
Time to grow and increase in power
But post separation abuse would lower

A single mum is now her status
They point and stare, do they really hate us?
To control the narrative he provides the gossips
fodder
Out to destroy he'll give no quarter
To keep control he manipulates the rules
Using police, social workers and courts like
fools

Now for years and years of court dates
Constant prayers to be saved fae the fates
Regular threats a kids taken away
Silenced when she tries to have her say
Be happy now ye've escaped she's telt
No acknowledgement that the control is still felt

Forgive and Forget

They say ye must forgive and forget
It's really the only way they will let
You must be a good Christian and offer
remission
No requirement for them to offer contrition
Please open your eyes and see they are usin
Your belief in forgiveness to continue abusin

When ye leave it's not the abuse ye are losin
But more the mode of control ye are movin
Ye see an abuser will say ye stole
Loss of his belongings he cannae thole
Disnae see ye as a person o yer ain
Just an object to destroy or regain

How can ye forget when ye need tae be watchin
On yer guard for the next plan he be hatchin
What is it yer meant tae forgive?
When he still expects that way ye tae live
When she has aready a massive price paid
Why on her should all the responsibility laid?

Resilience

Again they tell me to start being resilient
Always they ignore the points that are salient
Yes, I stopped and had a cry
But I got back up and continued to try
Yes, when I heard it knocked me back
But I got back up, not ignoring what I couldn't
hack
Yes, I felt the overwhelming fear
But I got back up and fought for what I held dear
Yes, people say I am not good enough
But I got back up and worked to adapt to times
tough
So to you what does resilience mean
Not the same as to me it would seem
You only focus on me being knocked down
Ignore that like Rocky, I got back up for the next
round

A Decent Mum

Noo listen carefully this can be confusin
No matter hoo lang this question ye've been
musing
Fir a tightrope ye must walk, a narrow path
If title o decent mum ye want tae have
Noo a day lang ye must be at hame
While earning loads in yer ain name
Cook a yer meals yersel from scratch
But no miss oot on the latest product, natch
Hair, nails and make-up perfectly done
Spend time on yersel, Well yer neglectsome
Teach yer kids everything ye can mind
But but let 'em play alone or they'll be behind
Pick them up in a nice, classy car
Just make sure ye didn't tak it too far
Spend plenty o money so nae body thinks yer
poor
While been prudent and savvy that's for sure
Take loads o holidays they must be abroad
But to slumming it at home ye must also gie a
nod
A decent mum must be like baby bear's porridge
Fir the Goldilocks judges are mighty savage.

It's Ower

"C'mon noo hen, it's ower ye've left"
"Dinnae understaun hoo ye can be bereft"
Ye wish and pray that that were true
As leaving ye begin tae rue
Ye may no longer be in punchin distance
But ye'll still suffer at his insistence
Social work he may gie a call
"she's the wurst mither o all"
Even the polis he may use
To continue on wi his abuse
Homicide timeline, he's approaching stage 81
Murder victim could be yer fate
That's something onybody wid fear
And isnae solved by "now now dear"
Instead he may employ the court, wi ony luck
But then for years per life will really suck
As tae his demands the court will pander
Wioot even givin yer evidence a gander
Time and money tae jump thru hoops
Set up tae fail, are they in cahoots?
Questioning will it ever end
As yer whole life ye defend
So noo dae ye get why she's bereft
Even less freedom noo she's left
IN even more fear o her life

Than ever she was durin the years o strife
Next time but she left ye wonder
Consider hoo her life's bee torn asunder
Yer intentions may have been on the side o right
But remember all ye did was gaslight

Scars You Cannot See

You'll have seen the classic abuse image
Cuts and bruises or even a bandage
But there are scars you cannot see
Abuse that changes who you will be
To control he would glare and shout
Or he may have banned you from going out
Dictated what you were to wear
Criticised your brains, figure and your hair
Every opportunity to put you down
Threats of reports to every agency in town
Makes a habit of being a liar
Many excuses he is a trier
Talks you into having his baby
Will he help? Only maybe
If you leave he'll demand copious contact
That he's the boss and unwritten contract
Treats you like his personal slave
Threats to put you in your grave
To rape he sees as his right
His self control will hide your plight
If one day you do now escape
Your world view you must now reshape
Adaptive changes made for survival
Those scars must heal for your revival

The Lecture

"Ye were abused, wur ye aye?
Bitch Please! That maun be a lie.
Pfft! That bruise is awfie wee
If real abuse abody would see
Oft! That black ee is a stoater
Moan be a fake ye self-promoter
If it's real, why do ye no greet
Ye urnae fitting the profile neat
Oh! Ye gret yester-een
Manipulation yer gie mean
Ah but he ne'r hit ye hen
Ye need controlled do ye no ken
Ye huvnae been an angel pure
Maybe ye deserved it, ur ye sure"

Ye got this far please haud ona mo
There's something ye really huv tae know
Ye may have guid reason fir the wirds abuin
A liar ye feel remains impune
The wirds ye say they soon gang fleeing
But the target isnae the wan who's seeing
As wirds spread faster than yon flu
A victim worries is that what happens if I tell
you
Really plants the seed o doubt

A'm a wrang tae be wanting out
Is whit's happenin abuse real
A'm a bad tae feel whit a feel
If this is whit a really deserve
Moan be morally wrang ma safety tae conserve

Noo it's clear they wurnae the target intended
But abuse trauma isnae easily mended
Their abuser their confidence did destroy
Little strength left for survival tae deploy
If in a bit o the rant they see themsel
Reinforce the abusers message to keep them in
hell
Whit we aw huv tae realise
Different disnae huv tae mean lies
Public words urnae a precise attack
As innocents get hit wi a lot o flack
Collateral damage, innocent victims distressed
By views of others loudly expressed.

Alone

The abuser he did isolate
To be alone it wis yer fate
But yersel ye could console
ithers hatred ye widnae huv tae thole
Auld friends exist only at airm's length
But their existence gies ye strength
Nae idea hou wrang ye coud be
One day their thocts ye'd huv tae see
When their hero took his ex tae court
They'd jamp tae let ye know whit they think o
yer sort
Tae Facebook, Twitter and tik tok they tak
themsel
Tae tell ye ye belang in hell
Sae clear ye noo can be sae suire
They think ye a bitch, an evil whore
"ye deserved it aw" they dae cry
As whit happened they also deny
Ye thocht ye felt alone afore
As you gret ahint a closed door
Noo the pain o being suroonded wi hate
Tae save yer kids it feels twa late
Noo, the friends ye must cut loose
En if they claim "but a dinnae mean youse"
Cause aye the did nae matter the denial

They didnae rectrict their comments tae wan
trial
Only when caught oot dae they backtrack
Yet willnae cut ye any slack
A they tell ye ye huv nae right
Tae be upset at their attacks forthright
Tis wan thing fir them no to help ye heal
Anither fir them tae want ye pain tae feel.

Witchhunt

We read the tale o Bessie Dunlop
Pourfu men decided she wis fir the chop
Burnt at the stake oan Castle Hill
Confessed to witchcraft against her will
Targeted cause she widnae play along
They couldnae thole a wummin strong
They micht say we progressed in the Victorian
age
But asylum registers page efter page
List weemen admitted fir the greater guid
Symptoms: thinking or talking mair than men
thocht they should
Aye weel they wurnae burnt at the stake
Jist locked up and tortured wi diagnoses fake
We pride oursel oan oor times progressive
No resorting tae these acts excessive
Well aye we nae longer get tried as a witch
Jist cry us a tart, wh**e or b**ch
The auld asylums they are lang closed
Instead Chemical restraints and discrediting
diagnoses are proposed
Every effort your voice to disable
Each time you try an bring yer views to the table
Ye se they call it a withhunt fir a reason

We've not progressed jist moved to a new
season.

16

Responsibility

"You! step up and take responsibility
You must be to blame, no other possibility
It may have been him who exerted control
But you being to blame is all we can thole
Remember dear he is a man
Supposed to keep him happy any way you can
We'll never accept that he is to blame
Else we'd have to accept that we could face the
same
Holding him responsible would be very hard
So truth of his guilt I must be very hard
So truth of his guilt I must disregard
I value men in charge, the order natural
You my dear are out of line, unnatural
Hearing your pain will cause discomfort and
hurt
So be responsible and keep your mouth shut
Remember it is the natural consequence
of being a victim of another's actions
Now one final responsibility you must take
All for my ego and comfort's sake
You must never breath a word
Of my demands no matter how absurd
Tua culpa, remember we must try
Constantly to perpetuate the abuser's lie

Someone must take responsibility
Never going to be the narcissistic personality"
Society will always take the easy way out
Use their numbers to retain clout
The one taking responsibility, the blame
and the guilty party are rarely the same

Punishment Enough

Keep your head down and toe the line
Let them pretend everything in the world is fine
All the abuse that you have faced
Their Rose tinted view it has defaced
For this punishment must be meted out
but not to the abuser! in case there's doubt
You made a mistake, wrong man you did chose
Love bombing, it did turn to abuse
No dear it wasn't punishment enough
When he tried to destroy your stuff
Nor when he split open your head
Definitely not when he wished you were dead
Not even when he hurt your kid
Nor when your security he got rid
Now dear more punishment you must face
To us, your existence is a disgrace
So now it's time for us to do our stuff
Hold on tight it may get rough
We will make sure you know your place
To feel the shame and hide your face
We'll begrudge you any success
Insist that you remain in distress
You must face the consequences of your mistake
Consideration for time served we will not take
We'll make sure you pay for life

While ensuring your abuser is free from strife

I Didn't Say

You don't understand why I didn't say?
Well a few things are at play
First what happened is hard to admit
Being in denial a more comfortable fit
He told me no one would believe me
And well, your postings, I did see
They suggested he was probably right
Telling you didn't seem worth the fight
I know you were talking about someone else
Ignorant that friends faced that themselves
Oh you say "I didn't mean youuuu!"
But those issues apply to me too
I've told you this but you still can't see
You've shown at best you won't believe me
You may even go on the attack
Ensure I can't get any dignity back
It feels safer to keep my mouth shut
If only to avoid adding to the hurt
It's clear he'll never be held to account
No matter how high the evidence may mount
I can never rely on you for support
I can tell from how you yourself comport
When faced with any victim's tale
To show understanding you repeatedly fail
Now do you understand today?

Why to YOU I'd never say

Austerity Season

How does one survive austerity season?
Ask the rich after all we're taught they're the
voice of reason
First switch aff yer second fridge
You ken, the one in your double garage
jist get yersel a second job at night
Already ha one, well get a 3rd awright
Fir yer holiday instead o 5 star
Settle for 3 ye can still go far
Fir yer daily Starbucks treat, here's a swap
Get yer own espresso machine, makes a fine
drap
Stap gan oot at night tae play
Ye don't? well stap it onyway
Ye must no have hame internet
The library we closed should be a safe bet
But what ye must remember above all
Ye must hold the rich in enthrall
As they enjoy the luxuries frae which yer
forbidden
Like heat, food and shelter, better stay hidden
So I can give you my very best tip
The only solution is to be born a VIP

Tae Buy a House

Here's the rules fir buying a hoose
Follow carefully and ye cannae loose
Move to here the work is plenty
While living with parents til way past 20
Miles to work ye must always walk
Think it's too far? Aboot laziness we must talk
Aim for promotion, arrive prim and proper
Wet or Windswept ye'll come cropper
Feel for saving ye need more wage
I hear second and third jobs are all the rage
Yer loads a free time get down to learning
Qualifications, so more ye'll be earning
But remember no student load or fees be
spending
Or mortgage companies will no be lending
Seriously ye must cut back on yer food
Want to be sated? well how rude!
Heat or eat a choice ye must make
Both luxuries ye really cannae take
Cancel every subscription, do what I say!
Don't hae them? well cancel them onyway
Follow every rile on this here list
No fund or rest I must insist
Keep it up non-stop for at least 10 year
And ye'll own a hoose by 21 no fear.

Just Learn Tae Cook

"They widnae struggle if they just learned tae
cook"
Annunciated the man with the haughty look
He obviously didnae think a Jenny the chef
She lost her job when COVID mean no business
left
Withoot a job and no earning money fir rent
Sitting in a B&B which by the cooncil she wis
sent

Limited fir noo in the temp accomodation
No kitchen so stuck in nutritional damnation
But the need fir energy is a necessity
If there's tae be a chance of a job in time of
scarcity
In spite of the struggles she does survive
She gets a flat, a time to thrive

Working long hours but pay is low
Progress building a kitchen is slow
Supermarket prices rising so high
That's when Jenny's life shines light on the lie
Fir Jenny already knows hoo tae cook it
Yet at the end of the month she is still rookit

Don't Do the Crime

Don't do the crime if you can't do the time
You'll have heard the oft quoted rhyme
But it doesn't give the picture full
Does it provide an accurate rule?
What time does the criminal actually serve?
While people make sure the victim gets what
they think they deserve
From now to forever seen as trouble
Trapped in a forever tightening bubble
"you must be more resilient you know"
As their needs and responsibilities they're
expected to forgo
Constant pressure to consider the criminal's
rights
While being called weak for all those sleepless
nights
Stand up and face then in the court
Judged on every word and how you deport
There's a need to find a better dictum
To recognise the punishment of the victim
Because time after time it is shown to be true
If you're a victim of crime, the one doing the
time is you

Finding a Voice

Silenced by him for years and years
as he controlled you by playing on your fears
Escape, time to find your voice and speak out
But then they'll fear you may gain clout
Told you must stay quiet and reserved
Your subservient position must be preserved
Told you must accept your shame
Make it clear it is you they blame
They try and stop you finding your voice
Stifling your ability, your freedom to rejoice
But it's just a matter of finding a way that's right
for you
To tell of your feelings and experiences true
It doesn't matter if they tell you you're rude
You may actually do some good
Help another victim feel less alone
Or to a doubter, bring the truth home
know it can help you at the very least
Your confidence and agency increased
Finding your voice your own value to learn
Is worth the effort this benefit to earn
Remember the only true benefactor of your
silence
Are the perpetrators of domestic violence
Hence the lesson is: your voice you should find

Even if only for your own peace of mind

28

Sacrifice

In Sparta back in days of old
We see on shields what their sons were told
"come back with this shield or on it"
Message to do or die was tacit
Then in enlightenment's age
A white feather sent by those who rage
At those they see as a pathetic coward
To fight and kill only way to be empowered
Then dulce et decorum est….
An instruction of what is for the best
Soon becomes a phrase on their epitaph
No life, just names read out at the cenotaph
Not yet past the age of sacrifice
As school children still give their life
Told must sacrifice for adult rights
Paying the price for others fights
A sacrifice is easy to make
When someone else the risk must take
May be the way it has always been
Not a valid reason it must be seen
Perhaps it's time to change our world view
Stop sacrificing our young for the glory of a
powerful few
Don't tell our young it's their duty, themselves
to martyr
Accept our duty to protect life for a starter.

9 789357 440851